The Scarecrows of Crowhill

Level 9 – Gold

Helpful Hints for Reading at Home

The graphemes (written letters) and phonemes (units of sound) used throughout this series are aligned with Letters and Sounds. This offers a consistent approach to learning whether reading at home or in the classroom.

HERE ARE SOME COMMON WORDS THAT YOUR CHILD MIGHT FIND TRICKY:

| water | where | would | know | thought | through | couldn't |
| laughed | eyes | once | we're | school | can't | our |

TOP TIPS FOR HELPING YOUR CHILD TO READ:

- Encourage your child to read aloud as well as silently to themselves.
- Allow your child time to absorb the text and make comments.
- Ask simple questions about the text to assess understanding.
- Encourage your child to clarify the meaning of new vocabulary.

This book focuses on developing independence, fluency and comprehension. It is a gold level 9 book band.

The Scarecrows of Crowhill

Written by Hermione Redshaw

Illustrated by Lily Fossett

Chapter One

Scared Crowhill

In the fields on the edge of Crowhill, an army of scarecrows defended the village. No crow dared fly down from the top of Crowhill Hill, not while the scarecrows were around.

They did not just defend against crows. There was no crime in Crowhill while the scarecrows stood guard. The villagers believed they were magic.

Then, one day, when everyone was going about their daily business, whispers began to make their way around the village. Soon, the news was everywhere. The unthinkable had happened. The scarecrows had vanished.

At school, everyone was talking about the missing scarecrows. The children had all sorts of tales about them from their parents and grandparents.

"The scarecrows are the magical protectors of Crowhill," said one.
"Bad things will happen if they don't return!" said another.

Hattie and Caleb did not believe them at first, but as they walked home from school…

The crows were like statues at first, still and silent. Then, one jumped when Caleb brushed past a fence. Next thing, hundreds of crows had taken flight! They were all over the village.

Finally, Hattie shouted to Caleb over the fluttering of wings, "We need to do something!"

Chapter Two

Missing Mobiles

The crow problem did not seem so bad after everyone woke up to find their mobile phones had gone missing. The villagers had to find new ways to talk to each other. Tin cans were tied together with string and strung all over the place. Paper aeroplanes with messages on them flew between houses.

"How will you find who did this now?" Hattie asked the police officer.
"Luckily, we use walkie talkies instead of phones," she replied.
"Do you have any spare?" asked Caleb, thinking about how useful they would be for their own investigation.

With their new walkie talkies, Hattie and Caleb split up to search the town.

Hattie went to school to interview their teacher, Miss Hayfield. She always hated phones, so she was a prime suspect.

"I've not missed phones in the classroom," Miss Hayfield said. "But I haven't been able to speak to my mum at all!"

Hattie thought about not being able to speak to her own mum every day. No one would want that. Miss Hayfield was clearly innocent.

Meanwhile, Caleb wandered the edge of the village.

"There are prints from boots in the mud around where the scarecrows used to be," he noticed.

He followed them as far as Crowhill Hill and stopped. Not even the crows wanted to go past the sign. Surely no one would go up there.

Hattie and Caleb told each other what they had found out over the walkie talkies.

Hattie remembered to include every detail. Caleb 'forgot' to mention about the prints leading to Crowhill Hill.

"I didn't find much," he said.

"There isn't anyone left to interview!" said Hattie. "I've spoken to them all. They're all innocent."
"So, what do we do?" Caleb asked. "Give up?"

Hattie did not want to give up.
"We'll decide tomorrow," she said. Maybe a new lead would appear overnight.

Chapter Three

The Blame Game

Since neither Hattie and Caleb, nor the police, had managed to solve the mystery, the villagers started blaming each other. Graffiti appeared on walls, saying things like, 'It was John!' and people were shouting at one another in the streets.

Eventually, the head of the village called a meeting in the square.

The whole village attended the meeting. However, Hattie's nan insisted that someone was missing.

Since Hattie had interviewed everyone yesterday, she knew this could not be true. The other villagers agreed with her.

"He used to live on the top of Crowhill Hill," said Nan.

"Impossible," said the postwoman. "I haven't delivered letters to Crowhill Hill in years!"
"Nobody lives up there but the crows," said the head of the village.

Except, the crows were not living on Crowhill Hill right now. Caleb decided then to tell Hattie about the prints in the mud.
"Whoever's been causing all this chaos must be at the top!" said Hattie.

Chapter Four

Crowhill Hill

Crowhill Hill was a very spooky place. It was no wonder Caleb was scared of it.

Fortunately, there was a road and Caleb's mum offered to drive him and Hattie as far as it went. They drove halfway up the hill before the road stopped. Mum turned off the engine. Hattie and Caleb got out.

"Here," said Caleb. He gave Mum his walkie talkie. "You're our backup if we need you."

"You'll be fine," said Mum. "I know Hattie's nan thinks someone lives up there, but she's mistaken."

It was a long, cold climb along a narrow lane up to the top of the hill, with steep drops either side. Soon, they were so high up that there was mist all around them. Hattie thought they had climbed into the clouds.

They came across no animals or flowers on their way up. In fact, they saw no signs of life at all, apart from each other.

"I don't like this," muttered Caleb, glancing this way and that.
"We're almost at the top," said Hattie.

However, the top was nowhere in sight because of all the mist.

Hattie and Caleb knew they had finally reached the top when they saw a roof poke out from the top of the hill. Then, the rest of an old house appeared. After that, they saw –
"The scarecrows!" Hattie cried.

In a large circle around the house stood every scarecrow that had gone missing from Crowhill.

"Now we know why the crows wouldn't come up here anymore," said Caleb.

Although they had found the scarecrows, there was no sign of anyone nearby. That did not matter, though. If Hattie and Caleb restored the scarecrows, the village would be saved.

Caleb decided not to call Mum on the walkie talkie to help them move the scarecrows. He wanted to surprise her. However, the scarecrows were heavier than they looked.

"Give me a hand?" he asked Hattie.

She joined him by the nearest scarecrow and together they lifted it out of the ground.

"Put that scarecrow down!"

The voice scared them. It came from the house. Hattie and Caleb kept hold of their scarecrow, but it was difficult. They were both shaking with fear.

A figure had appeared at the front door. The house was not abandoned after all.

Chapter Five
Old Mr Crow

An old man hobbled towards Hattie and Caleb. They were too scared to move as the man edged closer. He stopped in front of them.

"Y-y-you're the one who stole the scarecrows!" Hattie stammered.

"Mr Crow," the old man introduced himself. "I was hoping someone would come and visit me to look for them. No one has visited in years, or even sent a letter! Do you kids have any idea how lonely it's been?"

Hattie and Caleb explained to Mr Crow that no one knew he was there. They also told him how much chaos the crows had caused with the scarecrows gone.

Mr Crow looked guilty. He had not meant for any of that to happen.

"I'll help however I can," said Mr Crow.

He said he had not taken any phones, but he knew exactly who had.

"The crows love mobile phones!" said Mr Crow. "I've never kept one because of them!"

Hattie, Caleb and Mr Crow collected all the phones from the crows' nests and returned them to the villagers.

Everyone was delighted to see Mr Crow. They each gave him their phone number and told him to call any time.

Hattie and Caleb knew he would not be able to call anyone if the crows kept stealing his phone. So, when it came time to return the scarecrows, they left one where it was.

The Scarecrows of Crowhill

1. Why did Hattie think her teacher had stolen everyone's mobile phones?

2. Who drove Hattie and Caleb to the start of Crowhill Hill?

   a) Hattie's nan

   b) Caleb's mum

   c) The head of the village

3. What did Hattie and Caleb find on their scary journey up Crowhill Hill?

4. Mr Crow felt lonely at the top of Crowhill Hill. What does it mean to feel lonely?

5. How can you help someone who feels lonely? When have you helped someone like this?

©2022 **BookLife Publishing Ltd.**
King's Lynn, Norfolk, PE30 4LS, UK

ISBN 978-1-80155-806-8

All rights reserved. Printed in Poland.
A catalogue record for this book is available from the British Library.

The Scarecrows of Crowhill
Written by Hermione Redshaw
Illustrated by Lily Fossett

An Introduction to BookLife Readers...

Our Readers have been specifically created in line with the London Institute of Education's approach to book banding and are phonetically decodable and ordered to support each phase of Letters and Sounds.

Each book has been created to provide the best possible reading and learning experience. Our aim is to share our love of books with children, providing both emerging readers and prolific page-turners with beautiful books that are guaranteed to provoke interest and learning, regardless of ability.

BOOK BAND GRADED using the Institute of Education's approach to levelling.

PHONETICALLY DECODABLE supporting each phase of Letters and Sounds.

EXERCISES AND QUESTIONS to offer reinforcement and to ascertain comprehension.

BEAUTIFULLY ILLUSTRATED to inspire and provoke engagement, providing a variety of styles for the reader to enjoy whilst reading through the series.

AUTHOR INSIGHT:
HERMIONE REDSHAW

Hermione Redshaw has been writing books for over eight years, with a passion for adventure and fantasy. Her writing is often distinguished by themes of family and personal growth. Hermione holds a Bachelor's degree in English Language, Communication and Linguistics, with a keen interest in communicating difficult ideas in a clear and accessible way. Her Master's in Children's Publishing focused Hermione's experiments with bold and innovative concepts, from story apps to dyslexia-friendly and educational adventures. She joins BookLife Publishing with a drive to engage new and old readers alike.

This book focuses on developing independence, fluency and comprehension. It is a gold level 9 book band.